TERMS & CONDITIONS

COPYRIGHT © 2018 BY Shonda S. Caines

ALL RIGHTS RESERVED. YOU ARE WELCOME TO USE THIS PRODUCT FOR PERSONAL USE. OTHER THAN THAT, NO PART OF THIS PUBLICATION MAY BE REPRODUCED, STORED, OR TRANSMITTED IN ANY FORM OR BY ANY MEANS, ELECTRONIC, MECHANICAL, PHOTOCOPYING, RECORDING, SCANNING, OR OTHERWISE, EXCEPT AS PERMITTED UNDER SECTION 107 OR 108 OF THE 1976 UNITED STATES COPYRIGHT ACT, WITHOUT THE PRIOR WRITTEN PERMISSION OF THE AUTHOR. REQUESTS TO THE AUTHOR AND PUBLISHER FOR PERMISSION SHOULD BE ADDRESSED TO coach@awakenyourwellness.com

DEAR ADULT ©

INSIDER

TABLE OF CONTENTS

03 Foreword

04 Why Me?

05 Listen Up, Adults!

06 Learned Behavior

07 Deserved Protection

08 A Brand New Canvas

09 Workbook Questionnaire

13 Are You talking to your child?

16 Parents Take Action

24 Contact Information

FROM THE AUTHOR

SHONDA S. CAINES

WRITTEN BY S. CAINES

Who a child is conceived by makes up their DNA. What a child is birthed into molds their environment. What they're exposed to becomes their reality. Many, with the grace of God, are able to escape any chaos that becomes their perception of the world; however, a great deal of them don't escape.

Chaos has a tendency of growing up with them into adulthood, and unless accessed by a trained eye, it's seen as something without a root - one that's so deep, it's tied to a lineage that began decades ago.

So, today I am here with my reflection to adults, especially parents and guardians of God's most precious gifts- the children with silent souls searching for a space to thrive, grow, and evolve into the awesomeness God desires.

WHAT A CHILD IS BIRTHED INTO MOLDS THEIR ENVIRONMENT

DEAR ADULT | S. CAINES

Every child enters this world with the burdens of their ancestors already upon their life. However, there are some things the people responsible for caring for children should be aware of on a daily basis. Throughout this workbook, I'll share a few… and it will be made obvious why.

From the eyes of a child, they reflect and comprehend based on their current maturity. Hence, adults must be conscious of their behavior (or lack thereof) when they're within the presence of a child. I grew up in chaos. I am very grateful for where I am today and am one of the few who hasn't repeated my past. Glory to God!

Domestic Violence

What is domestic violence? How does it affect the family? Who suffers the most? What are the long-term effects on a child who is a product of an environment filled with violence within the family dichotomy? What are some traits they can pick up or shy away from?

As an adult putting pen to paper now, these are some questions that I have (I want to mention the questionnaire at the end here).

Why me? Why the burst of fighting when it appeared that the night was going to be a peaceful one?

I'm sure they piqued your interest, too. Well, I'm going to break it down from my point of view.

Presently over the age of 35, I coin myself as having lived a bit and through some storms - the biggest hurricanes I didn't want to wither through to reach land. Join me as I relive as much as possible…from the eyes of a child. Why me? Why the burst of fighting when it appeared that the night was going to be a peaceful one? Living in a full house can literally be a lot, even in a peaceful home. Some of us are wired to hunger for "me-time", silence, and a place to retreat as often as possible. Thanks to our unique make up, a great deal of us thrive in smaller groups. And yes, that includes our families. Well, I just made that up…but believe it to be true.

DEAR ADULT | S. CAINES

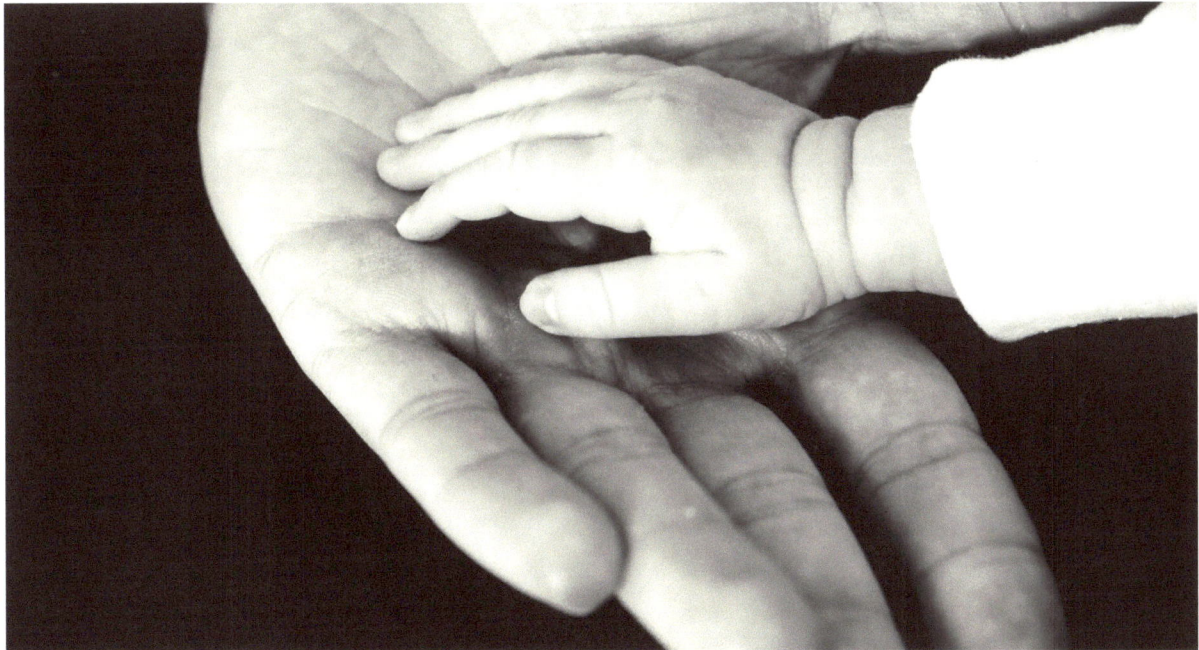

Perhaps they're drunk with restlessness from the night before, worried about their mom or dad being abused. Or, that unhealthy environment has adversely affected their diet.

Listen up, adults: Children need their sleep and need to know they're safe. They are of the utmost importance. Think about it: That might be a valid reason why so many children aren't good at focusing throughout the school day. Perhaps they're drunk with restlessness from the night before, worried about their mom or dad being abused. Or, that unhealthy environment has adversely affected their diet.

Thinking aloud now… Why do we have so many obese children in America? Is it because they're internalizing the chaos going on around them? Do they feel there's no one to express their feelings to and still return home without repercussions?

Listen up, adults: Children need their sleep and need to know they're safe.

Personally, I didn't feel there was such an outlet available for me. Seriously: Who can you turn to as a child? Then, as you get older and wiser, soon enough, you realize voicing your concerns can lead to the unweaving of the reality you know.

Will you be blamed for "destroying the family"? Will your siblings shun you? Will the parent you were most interested in shielding from harm disown you if his or her partner ends up in jail? And what about your grandmother (if she's somehow living nearby)? Will she understand what you did or only see it as a further destroying of the family? These are questions that occupied my young mind at one time or another.

Learned behavior

From the eyes of a child, dear parents: Children don't repeat what you say; they repeat what you do. Most often, if it's an unhealthy behavior, they have a habit of doing it 'better'. Don't believe me? Research how some of the most heinous crimes are committed by children who grew up in abusive environments. Take, for example, a son picking up the abusive behavior of his father. He now abuses his siblings and, most often, it's a sister. Why? He picked it up from his dad or stepdad. Later on, it can manifest to his girlfriend. You see, he didn't see boundaries and what love looked like from his primary male figure. His way of expressing himself was with abuse - and it comes in many forms.

Her face was always damp with tears, and his physical abuse was the cause. "How can you harm me while I'm holding your son - the child brought forth for you - while surviving distress by your hands? Besides, our older children and family members are witnessing this mistreatment!"

From the eyes of a child, dear adults, this hostile environment stays with us. It never goes away and is often times buried until something reminds us of the nightmares we endured. More often than not, we suffer in silence.

Sadly enough, boundaries were crossed and some children were abused - in more ways than one.

> Children don't repeat what you say; they repeat what you do. Most often, if it's an unhealthy behavior, they have a habit of doing it 'better'.

From the eyes of a child, who do you turn to? All you see are the adults within close proximity fighting, arguing, cursing at each other, crying, and fighting with children and others. For me, I turned to journaling my horrific childhood. I planned to share my journal with my dad but was fearful he'd request I live with him and, as a result, disrupt everyone's life.

From the eyes of a child, their cognitive skills are still being developed; their perception is magnified to a level of incomprehensibility by any adult. There's no way to rationalize the outcome in a positive light.

DEAR ADULT | S. CAINES

From the eyes of a child, we deserve to be protected, loved, and able to exist in an environment that's healthy.

Dear adults, please be cognitive of what you do around children. Does it matter if those children are yours? Absolutely not! This goes for parents, guardians, foster parents, grandparents, godparents, and relatives they spend time with. From the eyes of a child, we deserve to be protected, loved, and able to exist in an environment that's healthy. For a child, healthy means consistent, transparent, and inclusive. It also means supportive, fun, and memorable. I can't forget to mention that children want to feel safe and wanted. From the eyes of a child, adults tend to leave us out… and it hurts. We may be tiny; however, we are a part of the family, too.

So, you might ask me: How did you cope with the chaos around you? Well, while in middle school, on a trip to Toronto, Canada, I attempted to do the unthinkable.

I want you to think about what I'm referring to? I'll give you a minute…

It would pain any adult taking care of a child to hear they tried to do this: I tried to take my life by walking beyond the safety area of Niagara Falls.

So, with a still-developing brain, I concluded suicide would be the easiest way to handle all of that pressure. BUT - glory to God - my plan was foiled. A classmate of mine yelled out my name, which caught the attention of our chaperone who insisted I step back. That day on the bus, when we left the falls, I sat in silence thinking: Now what?

Well… No child should have their personal space invaded nor childhood stripped. From a child's eyes, sometimes we simply want someone to really stop and ask, "How are you doing?" - and mean it. We desire a safe haven in adults. We want our angels on earth. We expect someone to sense there's something wrong - and refuse to stop until it's exposed. We want at least one adult to think outside of the box, rather than labeling us as troublemakers. We want someone to have a discerning spirit.

DEAR ADULT | S. CAINES

From this child's eyes, there was now an opportunity to paint a brand-new canvas - one that had a home FILLED with calm, love, peace, consistency, and togetherness.

From this child's eyes, there was now an opportunity to paint a brand-new canvas - one that had a home FILLED with calm, love, peace, consistency, and togetherness. There were no areas for unhealthy energy by anyone. Still, I silently lived with deep scars. Though I was a college graduate, working a professional job, and living in a brand-new home bought without assistance from anyone but the Good Lord, the scars remained. There were signs of my past that kept haunting me. Sleep-walking and sleep-talking continued. Double-checking that the bedroom door was locked (although I lived alone) happened like clockwork.

Dear parents, what we endure as children is forever engrained within us. It goes so deep that our souls are pierced to a depth only God should reach. It took speaking with a sibling who also endured similar trauma and chaos to give me strength to release the past by finally speaking out. Therapy is necessary. It is very scary for those in need, but it must be done. Healing is a process, and it's forever evolving as the child transitions into adulthood and future stages of life. There will be triggers, but the pain isn't ours to keep hidden. God has us here for a reason. I'm grateful the cycle experienced as a child wasn't repeated as an adult.

Gifting my experiences to adults - From the Eyes of a Child - is with the hope that it helps save at least one child from witnessing or being wrapped up in abuse. Children are gifts, and a sacred space must be created to ensure they thrive and blossom into whatever God has for them to be and do. With sincere gratitude, I'm now able to help others realize healing is a must in order to embrace the scars and walk proudly across the battlefield. Their reality can help someone else!

FROM THE EYES OF A CHILD WORKBOOK QUESTIONNAIRE

HOW IS THE RELATIONSHIP WITH MY CHILD?

HAVE I CREATED A SPACE THAT WILL ALLOW MY CHILD TO TRUST ME WITH HIS OR HER MOST INTIMATE THOUGHTS AND IDEAS?

ARE MY RELATIONSHIPS POSITIVELY OR NEGATIVELY AFFECTING THIS CHILD?

_____
_____
_____
_____
_____
_____
_____

HAVE I ASKED HIM OR HER HOW THEY FEEL?

_____
_____
_____
_____
_____
_____
_____

HAS MY CHILD CHANGED LATELY?

_____
_____
_____
_____
_____
_____
_____

COULD I IDENTIFY THE ABUSE IF IT WAS UNDER MY OWN ROOF?

HOW IS OUR RELATIONSHIP SINCE MY LIFE CHANGED?

IS MY CHILD'S BEHAVIORAL CHANGES CONTINGENT UPON MY DOMESTIC RELATIONS?

_____
_____
_____
_____
_____
_____
_____

WHAT MESSAGES AM I SENDING MY CHILD BASED ON WHAT I ALLOW IN MY LIFE?

_____
_____
_____
_____
_____
_____
_____

WHEN WAS THE LAST TIME I HAD A QUALITY TALK WITH MY CHILD?

IF I HAVE EXPERIENCED ABUSE ON ANY LEVEL, HAS ANY HEALING TAKEN PLACE? IF NOT, HOW AM I REALLY FEELING?

WHAT ARE THE ADULT INFLUENCES AROUND MY CHILD? ARE THEY HEALTHY INFLUENCES?

_____
_____
_____
_____
_____
_____
_____

HAVE I DISCUSSED WITH MY CHILD WHAT HEALTHY AND UNHEALTHY BEHAVIORS ARE?

_____
_____
_____
_____
_____
_____
_____

HAVE I DISCUSSED WITH MY CHILD WHAT'S ACCEPTABLE AND UNACCEPTABLE BEHAVIOR? EXPLAIN WHY:

_____
_____
_____
_____
_____
_____
_____

DO WE HAVE AN OPEN RELATIONSHIP? (EXPAND ON WHAT YOU MEAN BY OPEN?)

_____
_____
_____
_____
_____
_____
_____

DOES MY CHILD VIEW ME AS A SAFE HAVEN?

_____
_____
_____
_____
_____
_____
_____

WOULD I WANT TO LIVE WITH "ME" IF I WAS A CHILD?

_____
_____
_____
_____
_____
_____
_____

Parents Take Action

NOW THAT YOU'VE ANSWERED THE QUESTIONS, HERE ARE ACTIONS YOU CAN IMPLEMENT TO DAY!

BE AWARE:

1. Based on my answers, am I fostering a healthy environment?

___

2. What actions and behaviors prove this to be true or false?

___

Parents Take Action

NOW THAT YOU'VE ANSWERED THE QUESTIONS, HERE ARE ACTIONS YOU CAN IMPLEMENT TO DAY!

BE UNDERSTANDING:

1. Your answers are the first step to change the trajectory and relationship.

2. Am I missing signs that are right in front of my face?
   How can I improve or change it?

DEAR ADULT PAGE 17

TAKE PRACTICAL STEPS:

1. Contemplate your truths to each question above.

2. Are your truths healthy?

3. Can I do this alone? What resources are available to me? Am I open to professional assistance and guidance? Am I ready, today?

Author's Final Reflection

My battle-scars have taught me compassion on a deeper level. I recognize and am constantly reminded that everyone is dealing with something they wish was only a bad nightmare. Today, I'm called to minister through holistic wellness and wholesome food as a Wellness Catalyst, Vegan Fitness Chef, Speaker, and Best-Selling Author. Today, we must kneel down and experience this life through the "Eyes of a Child" - and do right by them.

Who a child is conceived by makes up their DNA. What a child is birthed into molds their environment. What they're exposed to becomes their reality.

Together, let's protect our children by being aware, understanding…and practical. From my eyes, looking back as a child, I pray these words awaken each reader to the long-lasting and adverse effects abuse have on children. Abuse comes in many forms and, for a child, all abuse hurts - and shapes his or her reality all throughout adulthood.

Dear Adults, the eyes of a child are always on you. Make their reality as healthy and memorable as possible.

Question:

Would YOU want to live with YOU… from the eyes of a CHILD!

Shonda S. Caines

ABOUT

Shonda Caines is a Wellness Catalyst, Fitness Chef, Speaker and Best-Selling Author. After losing and keeping off 90 lbs, she strives to empower women to maximize their health and fitness. Through specialized programs and a holistic approach, she offers tools, tips and strategies to help clients Awaken Their Wellness. Shonda holds a Master of Public Administration and is a Certified Personal Trainer with certifications in Fitness Nutrition, Weight Loss and Group Exercise Instruction. A self-taught runner and cyclist, she went from nearly drowning in 2006 to learning how to swim and competing in a triathlon in 2012. Shonda is a frequent competitor in races from triathlons to marathons and is an RRCA Run Coach.

All of Shonda's race medals are reminders of how far she's come. Her most memorable race was the Old Glory 50 mile ultra marathon which taught her that when it comes to physical endurance, it's mind over matter. She says "I went from

daydreaming about losing weight on the couch to signing up for races and marathons. I can help you achieve your goals, too."

"Shonda was just what I needed to get back to feeling like my "old" self after having a baby. She has been a constant guide towards living a healthier/balanced life by challenging and encouraging me to improve my overall wellness".

-Joanna Haynes, Fitness Client

"Blessed I am to have met Ms. Caines as she has been such a phenomenal inspiration to both my young son and I!"

-Maliaka Huntley, Fitness Client

REFLECTIONS

REFLECTIONS

REFLECTIONS

CONTACT INFORMATION

For Assistance with:

- Awakening your wellness
- Eating healthier to reach your overall goals
- Help releasing what's weighing you down

Please connect with me!

I look forward to helping

YOU

become the healthiest you!

Wellness Catalyst | Fitness Chef | Speaker | Author

IG: shonda_caines

FB: shondascaines

Twitter: @shondacaines

LinkedIn: Shonda Caines

Website: www.shondascaines.com

**Email:
Coach@awakenyourwellness.com**

www.ingramcontent.com/pod-product-compliance
Lightning Source LLC
LaVergne TN
LVHW071031070426
835507LV00002B/113